Grace        myatt

M000313915

# 24 and 23 Make Me

Written & Illustrated by Julia Sacha

Edited by Merrie Koester Southgate

A Read for Science Publication

Copyright 2013 Julia Sacha

All rights reserved. No part of this publication may be reproduced or transmitted in any form or by any means, electronic or mechanical, including photocopy, recording, or any information storage and retrieval system, without permission in writing from the publisher.

Summary: Grace, who has Down's Syndrome, teaches the reader the genetic reason she came to be so "special". [Schools—Nonfiction 2. Life Science.] Sacha, Julia.

ISBN 978-0-9845419-1-1

Read for Science Publishing

www.readforscience.com

# ACKNOWLEDGMENTS

I would like to thank Merrie Koester Southgate for her motivation and encouragement during this project. She taught me that there was only one way to do something, and that was the right way. I would like to acknowledge Grace and her Mom for their support and enthusiasm. I would also like to thank my parents, Dennis and Denise Sacha, and my sister, Chris, for their never-ending love and inspiration.

Hi, I'm Grace.

It doesn't matter which of my 100 trillion body cells you look at—my fingernail, my heart, stomach, or my lungs.

My cells differ from yours in one important way.

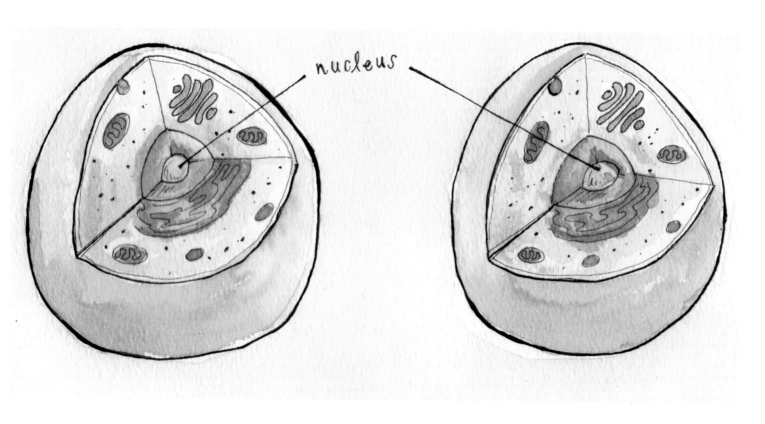

Can you tell one of your cells from mine?

You will if we zoom into the nucleus of each of our cells.

Inside the nucleus, you *should* find 23 pairs of structures called CHROMOSOMES, one from each of your parents.

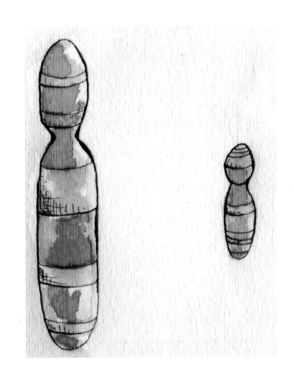

Chromosome 1 is the largest.

Chromosome 21 is the smallest.

The colored bands are called GENES. They have instructions for making everything in your body!

# Let's compare *your* chromosome pairs...

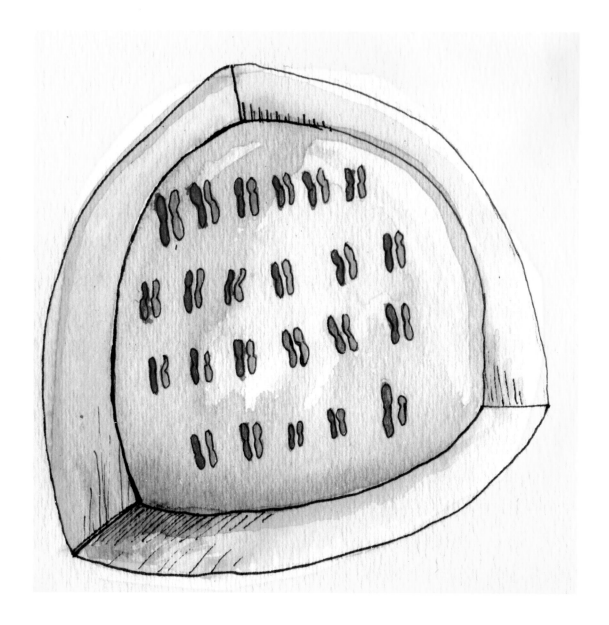

with mine.

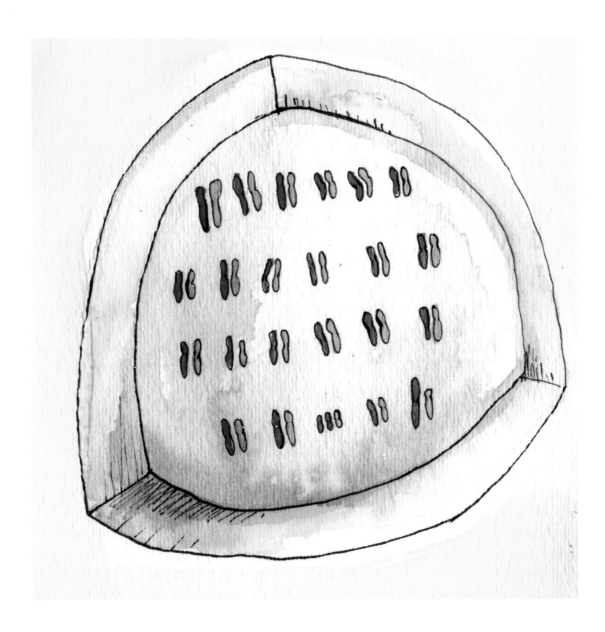

My cells have THREE 21$^{st}$ chromosomes, when they should only have TWO, like YOU!

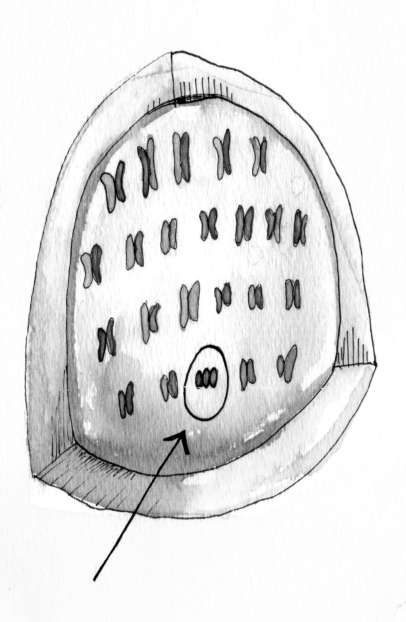

How did this happen?

It all started with a
process called
MEIOSIS.

In meiosis, your Mom's ovaries make round cells called EGGS,

while your Dad's testes make special swimming cells called SPERM.

But, unlike all your other body cells, eggs and sperm should only have 23 SINGLE chromosomes, *not* 23 pairs.

That way, when they come together, you start your life as a single cell called a ZYGOTE, with 46 chromosomes.

Every one of your 100 trillion cells came

from this one cell!

In my case, however, the egg that made *me* ended up with an *extra* 21st chromosome.

Let's use pipe cleaners to show what *should* happen to chromosome 21 during meiosis.

First, the immature egg, or OOCYTE, makes a copy
of each of its 23 pairs of chromosomes. Each copy is
joined to its "twin". The "foursome", or tetrad, then
moves toward the center of the nucleus.

Here, my fingers represent special fibers that pull the tetrad apart toward opposite sides of the cell.

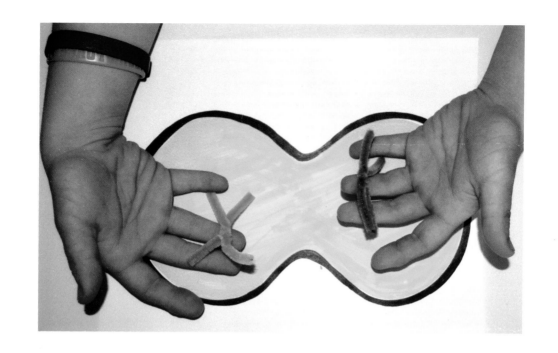

Next, the cell pinches in and pulls apart into 2 new cells.

Now, it's time to repeat the process!

The cells don't divide evenly, however.  Only
one gets to be THE EGG.

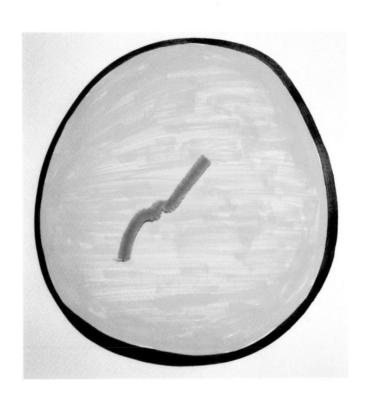

Remember, an
egg is only
supposed to
have ONE copy
of each
▨▨▨▨ ▨▨▨ ▨▨

But like I said, "I'm special!"

The egg that joined my father's sperm ended up after meiosis with TWO copies of chromosome 21.

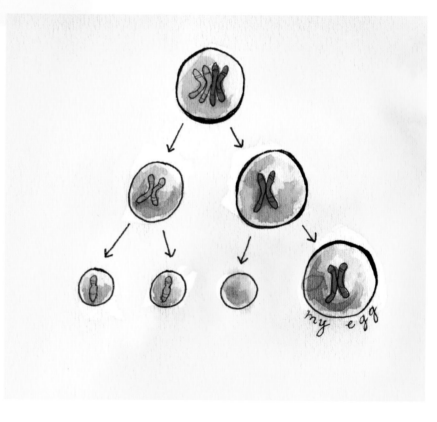

That extra 21st chromosome makes me special
in lots of ways:

- My eyes look like
  they're pushed up.

- I have a small mouth
  and small ears.
- I have little hands.

- I'm shorter than you.

# It even affects my health!

I am more likely to have:

Poor vision & hearin loss.

Breathing problems.

Heart defects.

Intestinal problems.

I may be different from you,
but that is *why* I'm so special.

Let's go have fun!